what did you received today ? ☺

DATE: /   /

Country:

I0481956

what did you received today ? ☺

DATE: /   /
Country:

what did you received today ? ☺

DATE: /   /
Country:

what did you received today ? ☺

DATE: /   /
Country:

what did you received today ? ☺

DATE: /   /
Country:

what did you received today ? ☺

DATE: /   /
Country:

what did you received today ? ☺

DATE: /   /
Country:

what did you received today ? ☺

DATE: /   /
Country:

what did you received today ? ☺

DATE: /   /
Country:

what did you received today ? ☺

DATE: /   /
Country:

what did you received today ? ☺

DATE: /   /
Country:

what did you received today ? ☺

DATE: /   /
Country:

what did you received today ? ☺

DATE: /   /
Country:

what did you received today ? ☺

DATE: /   /
Country:

what did you received today ? ☺

DATE: /   /
Country:

what did you received today ? ☺

DATE: /   /
Country:

what did you received today ? ☺

DATE: /   /
Country:

what did you received today ? ☺

DATE: /   /
Country:

what did you received today ? ☺

DATE: /   /
Country:

what did you received today ? ☺

DATE: /   /
Country:

what did you received today ? ☺

DATE: /   /
Country:

what did you received today ? ☺

DATE: /   /
Country:

what are you received today ? ☺

DATE: /   /
Country: